285 Miles of Prayer

A Memoir of My Six-Day Bicycle Sabbath Tour Through Southeast Georgia

Jeremy Cole

For reproduction permission, contact the publisher:

Tree Shadow Press

www.treeshadowpress.com

ISBN-13: 978-1-948894-09-8

DEDICATION

This humble testimony is dedicated my wife Amber.
Without her support, prayers, and patience,
I would have never been able to be on this journey called ministry.

ACKNOWLEDGMENTS

With gratitude to my friend Conn who braved this journey with me. Great thanks to the kind motorists of Southeast Georgia who gave us at least three feet when they passed us. To Amanda, Jim, Elise, and Gray for their hospitality in Glennville. To Allison and Griff for their hospitality in Douglas. Lastly, to my Aunt Debbie in her kind efforts to make this humble book possible.

All Scripture verses are from the
New International Version (NIV) Bible.

FEBRUARY 16, 2020

It's about 1:30 pm in Ludowici Georgia. I'm soaked from head to toe and shivering. I'm standing outside under a gas station awning clutching a large hot coffee, celebrating the nineteen rain-soaked miles from Glennville, trying to warm up for the next fourteen.

Conn is with me and we are grinning from ear to ear because we feel like superheroes after a war winning victory. This time yesterday, we felt like failures as we battled hill after hill and strong wind after strong wind. We crawled only thirty miles in the span of five hours. Today we blasted through 19, soaking wet in only an hour and a half. We're over halfway to our destination for the day, only 14 more rainy miles to go. We've got this!

MID-JUNE 2019

Almost five years ago I answered the call to ministry and applied to be the Director of Youth Ministries at St. Marys United Methodist Church in St. Marys Georgia. My call was planted in the summer of 2002 when I remember first saying out loud to a mentor and pastor, Reverend Rick Douylliez, that I thought I wanted to be a youth pastor. I was only sixteen and a youth myself, quickly experiencing a soul transformation on a mission trip in Appalachia. I may have been terribly young, naïve and unprepared, but a seed truly was planted. The germination, however, would last almost the next decade and a half.

In June of 2014 I was twenty-nine years old. I had been living back in St. Marys now for about three years. Over this time, I became very active in the leadership of the church that raised me. I taught Sunday school for pre-school age children. I served on nominating committees. I volunteered with the youth ministry under a great friend and youth pastor then, Luke Fox. I even served a half term as the church Lay Leader. My term was a half term because in just one month Luke would be putting in his resignation and answering a call to a different church ministry. Since Luke and I were so close, I knew about this before anyone else. I also was privileged to know so soon because he saw God nurturing the calling in me. It was just a year before this that

Luke and I had a late-night conversation about my calling at a BBQ competition in which he encouraged me and affirmed my call into ministry. Luke encouraged me to get my resume ready and apply for his soon to be vacated position. So, I did. I was on the church human resources committee and was awaiting the notice from the chair of that committee preparing us to begin the search for candidates to fill Luke's position. In almost a humorous way, I replied to that email with my resume attached. A few interviews, a conversation with my current employer, tears shed with my wife, and phone call later, I was the new Director of Youth Ministries for St. Marys United Methodist Church beginning August 1, 2014. To date, it's one of the scariest "yeses" I've ever yessed.

So here I was, a month to prepare for a job I had barely any idea of doing, and to start, I was only doing it part time while fading out of my other position. Early on, I was so insecure. I was second guessing myself at every possible opportunity.

Did I preach well?

Did I preach long enough?

Are the kids having fun?

Do the volunteers like me?

How do I do this better?

Encouragement from family, dedicated team members that made up our volunteers, an overwhelmingly supportive senior pastor that saw nothing but raw potential, and God's unfailing love got me through. That first year I received some training from National Youth Workers Convention, Download Youth Ministry Podcast, and a few great mentors

(Luke Fox and Jason Scott). All of this gave me a refined fire and drive to grow the ministry even better the next year. The next two years I continued to go to National Youth Workers Convention, soaking up all the great training it had to offer. Somewhere during this span, I made prayer a priority. I joined a morning prayer group, began keeping a prayer journal, and intentionally prayed before every program event we had. I saw immediate growth that can only be accredited to the power of prayer. I continue to make prayer a top priority today.

The next two and half years, I began attending this amazing thing called Orange Conference. The whole mission and message behind the Think Orange movement has been a ministry and faith walk game changer. Imagine what your own life and ministry could be like if you took every moment possible to value and lift up the next generation and your fellow human in the overwhelming unconditional love of Christ? That's what Orange has done for me. It would honestly take a separate book to explain what Orange is all about in detail. Lucky for you, it already exists.

Check out www.thinkorange.com for more information.

Over the last five years of ministry and just living life, I've come across some challenges I didn't think I ever would encounter.

In November of 2017 one of our youth lost one of her best friends to suicide and I did my best to minister to her through that.

In June of 2018 I lost a close friend and mother of two of our youth to suicide, just days after returning from our summer mission trip. I wept through scripture reading at her funeral. I still can't read Romans 8:38-39 or Psalm 23 without getting even a little choked up.

I came dangerously close to having a drinking problem and got sober now for over two years.

My wife and I struggled with infertility and began exploring the process to become foster parents.

And now here we are at Mid-June 2019.

My mother-in-law has been admitted to the hospital and the doctors have found two areas of tumors. She has one in her lung and three in her brain. They're going to operate.

My wife and family are scared about what's next. So am I, but I've got to be strong for my wife, for my father-in-law, for my brother-in-law, for my sweet nieces. I've never had ministry or life challenge quite like this

JULY 3, 2019

Treatment is going well for my mother-in-law. The surgeons removed most of the brain tumors and she's recovering well. The next steps will be radiation and then possibly chemotherapy.

I've been riding my bike a lot lately. I'm finding it's a great way to escape all the business of life and ministry and just get some good quiet reflection with God. I think I need some sort of extended time on the bike, like a several day tour. I'm close to several state parks and I could easily rig up the bike to carry camping gear. I think I'll explore a potential route.

I spent a few hours today mapping out a six-day bike tour through southeast Georgia. I plan to start here at home and go to Laura Walker State Park, then General Coffee State Park, then Gordonia Alatamaha State Park, then Happy Camper's RV Park in Hinesville, then Brunswick, then home. I posted the following photo to Instagram and got a lot of encouragement. My mother-in-law even said she'd like to go when she gets better.

 **jeremyscottcole**   ...

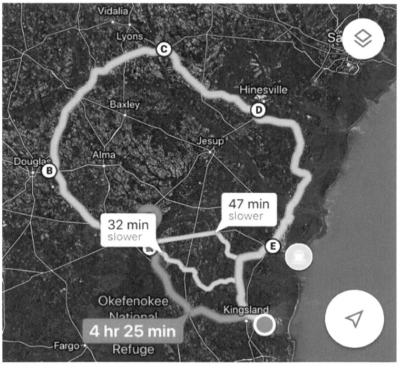

 Liked by **lordlover24** and **others**

jeremyscottcole Gonna start training for a 6 day sabbath
bike trip.
A. Laura Walker State Park
B. General Coffee State Park
C. Gordonia-Alatamaha State Park
D. Happy Campers RV Park Hinesville Ga
E. Blythe Island Regional Park
F. Home
#ridefatmanride

CANCER SUCKS

Radiation treatments took a severe drain on my mother-in-law. She became weaker and weaker very quickly. In mid-July she went in for a PET scan and we waited to receive the results. It was almost the first week of August when she went in for another radiation treatment and to receive the PET scan results.

The cancer was everywhere. She was getting weaker and weaker and it was harder and harder see her go through this terrible thing. Maybe even harder to see my family hurt through it all. She came home from the last radiation on a Friday, was helped to bed where my father-in-law didn't leave her side, and she went home to Jesus that Monday.

More and more the need for a more intentional time away with God is become more needed. Ministry is hard enough, and I need a recharge from that, but this year! We're still waiting for foster care approval. We've lost my mother-in-law. And the wheels of life don't stop turning for anyone.

Over the rest of the year it was time for the "firsts." The first birthday without her, the first Thanksgiving without her, the first Christmas without her, the first… everything without her. Lord give us your mercy! I need to get away with you.

So, throughout the year I continued to plan. I set a date for the trip, February 13-18, 2020. I got a good friend to do the trip with me. I trained, putting in longer rides as often as I could, even doing two 60+ mile rides. I got ready. I prayed. I planned. I packed. Over Christmas, I asked friends and family to give me scripture verses that I could use as my devotion time on the trip and outlined them each day in my journal.

As the days kept counting down to the trip, the more and more I was affirmed that I needed it. I needed to recharge.

I'm reminded of the time Jesus fed the 5000 and what he does immediately after feeding everyone, possibly his greatest miracle, is he goes up the mountain to pray. He needed intentional recharging and so do I.

So here I am now.

The day is almost here. I felt it was important to know the why (everything before all this) before I tell the story of the trip. Are you ready for a life changing six-day journey of twists, turns, blessings and challenges?

Here we go, friend.

FEBRUARY 13, 2020 (AM)

Jeremiah 29:11

*[11] For I know the plans I have for you,"
declares the LORD, "plans to prosper you and not to harm
you, plans to give you hope and a future.*

Proverbs 3:5-6

*[5] Trust in the LORD with all your heart
and lean not on your own understanding;
[6] in all your ways submit to him,
and he will make your paths straight.*

The day has come. Months of planning, a year of growth, a year of an emotional roller coaster… But you're here God. You've been here ordering my steps and preparing the way. It's 59.5 miles to Laura Walker State Park – Speak Lord, your servant is listening.

I pray for safety, endurance, fair weather, and kind travelers. Thank you for this gift Lord. I'm ready. Open my heart to know and reach the plans you have for me. I'm trusting you Lord. Lead me now into the first long miles of stillness.

FEBRUARY 13, 2020 (PM)

Psalm 42

For the director of music. A maskil of the Sons of Korah.
¹ As the deer pants for streams of water,
so my soul pants for you, my God.
² My soul thirsts for God, for the living God.
When can I go and meet with God?
³ My tears have been my food
day and night,
while people say to me all day long,
"Where is your God?"
⁴ These things I remember
as I pour out my soul:
how I used to go to the house of God
under the protection of the Mighty One
with shouts of joy and praise
among the festive throng.
⁵ Why, my soul, are you downcast?
Why so disturbed within me?
Put your hope in God,
for I will yet praise him,
my Savior and my God.
⁶ My soul is downcast within me;
therefore I will remember you
from the land of the Jordan,
the heights of Hermon—from Mount Mizar.

7 Deep calls to deep
in the roar of your waterfalls;
all your waves and breakers
have swept over me.
8 By day the LORD directs his love,
at night his song is with me—
a prayer to the God of my life.
9 I say to God my Rock,
"Why have you forgotten me?
Why must I go about mourning,
oppressed by the enemy?"
10 My bones suffer mortal agony
as my foes taunt me,
saying to me all day long,
"Where is your God?"
11 Why, my soul, are you downcast?
Why so disturbed within me?
Put your hope in God,
for I will yet praise him,
my Savior and my God.

Thank you, Lord, for this word. Thank you for leading me all the way here. It's been a blessed day. I've seen your beauty and wonder in the forests, the kind people I met, everything. Thank you for strength to do this. Lord this word today speaks to my weariness to seek after you. Please bless this small cottage we have for the night. Thank you so much Lord.

I began the day around 8:30 am from Kingsland First United Methodist. I pedaled hard, maybe too hard north on US 17 to Waverly. I ordered two sparkling waters from the

Waverly Minit Mart and rested at what's known as "The Hitchhiker's Table."

I had been itching to go all week. I think excitement got the best of me for pacing myself. I pedaled hard again down GA 110 West and made it to US 82 in Atkinson where I stopped for lunch at The Village Snack Bar.

The lady who worked the window was so nice. I ordered a large cheeseburger, small fry (which was huge), and a strawberry shake. She asked where I came from, where I was going and why I was doing it.

I told her, "Kingsland to all over southeast Georgia with Laura Walker State Park as the destination today." I continued, "I'm a pastor and It felt like it was time for something like this."

She smiled and said, "I wish more folks in the church would do something like that. Everybody is too busy and can't slow down."

I thanked her and waited for my lunch. It was DELICIOUS! I thanked her again, refilled my water bottles and headed west on US 82.

US 82 was windy. I've ridden in my share of wind but I'd never experienced wind like this while riding. My average speed of 14.5 mph on US 17 and GA 110 was slowed down to 6-9 mph at best. I was in for a crawl. A handful of times a gust almost blew me off the road. The last twenty-five miles of today's journey drug on. I stopped to rest several times. Each time, checking the GPS to be stunned that I had only traveled a few more miles.

My friend Terry, who owns Camden Bicycle Center, told me that church hoses and spigots are great places to refill water bottles. I took a Nahunta church up on that and rested a while against their sanctuary doors.

The whole time against the wind I just knew I could make it. I knew God would keep giving me the strength. Finally, I made it to Laura Walker State Park. I checked in and came outside to a downpour. I guess that explains the wind. It was just a preview to what was behind it.

I had checked into tent camping. As I sat on the porch of the park office waiting for a clear break in rain to go set up camp, I dosed off. When I woke, rain hadn't stopped. So, I went inside the office with only five minutes to spare and paid $16 more for a camper cabin. Conn arrived and we had dinner. We caught up with each other since the last time we were together and settled in until the morning.

Tomorrow we're off to General Coffee State Park in Douglas Georgia.

Departure from Kingsland First United Methodist Church.

The Village Snack Bar, Atkinson, GA

Camper Cabin, Laura Walker State Park

FEBRUARY 14, 2020 (AM)

Ephesians 2:8-10

*⁸ For it is by grace you have been saved, through faith —
and this is not from yourselves, it is the gift of God —
⁹ not by works, so that no one can boast. ¹⁰ For we are
God's handiwork, created in Christ Jesus to do good
works, which God prepared in advance for us to do.*

1 Peter 5:7

⁷ Cast all your anxiety on him because he cares for you.

Thank you for this word this morning. Lord, I hear you saying to rejoice in your love, grace, and strength. I hear you calling me to cast the cares of this day on you. Thank you for a great night's rest, hearty breakfast, my travel companion Conn, and the day ahead. Please keep us safe as we travel today.

FEBRUARY 14, 2020 (PM)

Psalm 51

¹ Have mercy on me, O God,
according to your unfailing love;
according to your great compassion
blot out my transgressions.
² Wash away all my iniquity
and cleanse me from my sin.
³ For I know my transgressions,
and my sin is always before me.
⁴ Against you, you only, have I sinned
and done what is evil in your sight;
so you are right in your verdict
and justified when you judge.
⁵ Surely I was sinful at birth,
sinful from the time my mother conceived me.
⁶ Yet you desired faithfulness even in the womb;
you taught me wisdom in that secret place.
⁷ Cleanse me with hyssop, and I will be clean;
wash me, and I will be whiter than snow.
⁸ Let me hear joy and gladness;
let the bones you have crushed rejoice.
⁹ Hide your face from my sins
and blot out all my iniquity.
¹⁰ Create in me a pure heart, O God,
and renew a steadfast spirit within me.

¹¹ *Do not cast me from your presence*
  or take your Holy Spirit from me.
¹² *Restore to me the joy of your salvation*
  and grant me a willing spirit, to sustain me.
¹³ *Then I will teach transgressors your ways,*
  so that sinners will turn back to you.
¹⁴ *Deliver me from the guilt of bloodshed, O God,*
  you who are God my Savior,
and my tongue will sing of your righteousness.
¹⁵ *Open my lips, Lord,*
  and my mouth will declare your praise.
¹⁶ *You do not delight in sacrifice, or I would bring it;*
  you do not take pleasure in burnt offerings.
¹⁷ *My sacrifice, O God, is a broken spirit;*
  a broken and contrite heart
  you, God, will not despise.
¹⁸ *May it please you to prosper Zion,*
  to build up the walls of Jerusalem.
¹⁹ *Then you will delight in the sacrifices of the righteous,*
  in burnt offerings offered whole;
  then bulls will be offered on your altar.

This word today God! "Create in me a clean heart."

I feel like that is happening for me mile after mile.

Thank you for this day. Thank you for getting us here just in time. Thank you for strength of each mile. Your love is enduring. I feel your grace and strength.

We began today around 11:00 am and headed west on US 82. We had to wait out the rain. Our first stop was Huddle House in Waycross. We both had patty melts and fries. The waitress was nice, and the lunch hour crowd was lively.

We made our way west on Albany Street that paralleled US 82 but was lighter trafficked. We followed this all the way through the industrial part of downtown until it merged back into US 82. From there, we planned to connect on GA 158, but GA 158 was closed, and we were directed to detour several miles. We scouted Google Maps and decided on a route made of several country roads (all of which appeared to be paved).

We were mistaken. Two of the roads we chose were partially dirt, one for nearly ten miles.

We finally made it to GA 32 just before dusk. Only 2.6 miles to go.

Dirt roads are tough and slowed us by half of our normal pace. We stopped often to encourage each other, snack, and hydrate. A good friend met us at the campsite with a BBQ dinner. We set up camp with head lamps, took showers and are settling in for the night. It was better today with a friend by my side. Christian fellowship has a way of doing that for us.

Day 2 Departure from Laura Walker State Park.
Jeremy (left), Conn (right).

Resting at the detour sign that led to us re-routing the trip.

Dirt Road just south of General Coffee State Park

Dinner compliments of Allison and Griff

FEBRUARY 15, 2020 (AM)

2 Corinthians 4:16

*16 Therefore we do not lose heart. Though outwardly we
are wasting away, yet inwardly we are being
renewed day by day.*

Romans 8:38-39

*38 For I am convinced that neither death nor life, neither
angels nor demons, neither the present nor the
future, nor any powers, 39 neither height nor depth, nor
anything else in all creation, will be able to separate us
from the love of God that is in Christ Jesus our Lord.*

Reflection and renewal; that is what I hear you speaking to me this morning. I also hear the truth of your unfailing love that will guide me today. Thank you for rest. Thank you for a great breakfast. We've got 66 miles ahead of us today. Lord bless and order our steps.

FEBRUARY 15, 2020 (PM)

Psalm 56

¹ *Be merciful to me, my God,*
for my enemies are in hot pursuit;
all day long they press their attack.
² *My adversaries pursue me all day long;*
in their pride many are attacking me.
³ *When I am afraid, I put my trust in you.*
⁴ *In God, whose word I praise—*
in God I trust and am not afraid.
What can mere mortals do to me?
⁵ *All day long they twist my words;*
all their schemes are for my ruin.
⁶ *They conspire, they lurk,*
they watch my steps,
hoping to take my life.
⁷ *Because of their wickedness do not let them escape;*
in your anger, God, bring the nations down.
⁸ *Record my misery;*
list my tears on your scroll—
are they not in your record?
⁹ *Then my enemies will turn back*
when I call for help.
By this I will know that God is for me.
¹⁰ *In God, whose word I praise,*
in the LORD, whose word I praise—

¹¹ in God I trust and am not afraid.
What can man do to me?
¹² I am under vows to you, my God;
I will present my thank offerings to you.
¹³ For you have delivered me from death
and my feet from stumbling,
that I may walk before God
in the light of life.

Your word tonight Lord is again so timely. All through our lives there are powers working against us. Some come in the form of others trying to tear us down, and some are physical struggles. Through it all, you are with us Lord. Your promise endures the whole way. Thank you for the amazing blessing of the day. You carried us through. You sent us help. You empowered the helpers. Praise and thanks are yours forever.

We got a later start than we'd like today. We had a steady momentum for the first 15 miles or so. Hills were tough, but the wind was gentle. We enjoyed lunch at a great little place called Big Ben's in West Green about 9 miles from last night's camp. I had a fried steak sandwich. Conn had a deli ham sandwich.

Over the next 21 miles we encountered challenging hills and strong winds that slowed us down dramatically.

We reached Hazlehurst at 2:30 pm, assessed the rest of the day and knew we would run out of daylight before we could reach Reidsville.

So, I called a pastor friend in Glennville (40 miles away)

to see if they'd come take us to our destination. They offered up something better and took us to Glennville. From there, they treated us to dinner at The Rusty Pig and checked us into a hotel.

Sometimes God's wisdom redirects our path and sends us kind angels to help. It's hard to not feel like a failure for falling short on the intended journey today, but I fully trust that all of this was part of the plan all along. Knowing and trusting that this was part of God's will for the sabbath journey turns this feeling of failure into one of joy and thanksgiving. Tomorrow we will press on hard thirty-three miles to Jesup right after worship with our friends.

One of our many rest stops just south of Hazlehurst, Ga

The great Hazlehurst rescue of Amanda and Gray!

Hotel in Glennville with gracious thanks to
Jim, Amanda, Elise and Gray

FEBRUARY 16, 2020 (AM)

Galatians 6:9-10

[9] Let us not become weary in doing good, for at the proper time we will reap a harvest if we do not give up. [10] Therefore, as we have opportunity, let us do good to all people, especially to those who belong to the family of believers.

Thank you for this word this morning. I thank you for those who have "done good" to us along the way. I thank you again for this sabbath journey to renew me for "doing good" and caring for the least of these. I pray blessing on the ride today. Please keep away the rain, give us light and kind traffic and keep us safe and joyful through the journey. If we have opportunity today, let us be able to return the generosity given to us.

Thank you Lord.

FEBRUARY 16, 2020 (PM)

Psalm 91

¹ *Whoever dwells in the shelter of the Most High*
will rest in the shadow of the Almighty.
² *I will say of the LORD, "He is my refuge and my*
fortress,
my God, in whom I trust."
³ *Surely he will save you*
from the fowler's snare
and from the deadly pestilence.
⁴ *He will cover you with his feathers,*
and under his wings you will find refuge;
his faithfulness will be your shield and rampart.
⁵ *You will not fear the terror of night,*
nor the arrow that flies by day,
⁶ *nor the pestilence that stalks in the darkness,*
nor the plague that destroys at midday.
⁷ *A thousand may fall at your side,*
ten thousand at your right hand,
but it will not come near you.
⁸ *You will only observe with your eyes*
and see the punishment of the wicked.
⁹ *If you say, "The LORD is my refuge,"*
and you make the Most High your dwelling,
¹⁰ *no harm will overtake you,*
no disaster will come near your tent.

¹¹ For he will command his angels concerning you
to guard you in all your ways;
¹² they will lift you up in their hands,
so that you will not strike your foot against a stone.
¹³ You will tread on the lion and the cobra;
you will trample the great lion and the serpent.
¹⁴ "Because he loves me," says the LORD, "I will rescue
him;
I will protect him, for he acknowledges my name.
¹⁵ He will call on me, and I will answer him;
I will be with him in trouble,
I will deliver him and honor him.
¹⁶ With long life I will satisfy him
and show him my salvation."

Thank you Lord for getting us through the challenge today. Thank you for safety, no mechanical trouble, gentle hills, kind motorists, light traffic and the strength to make it through. This word today God, is perfect. The only way we made it today is through our hope in you. You kept us safe. You helped us conquer. You gave us the strength. Thank you Lord for this amazing day.

After a great night's rest in Glennville, we began the day in worship with our friends at Glennville First United Methodist. All night before we went to best, we continued to check the weather and prayed for the rain to disappear. This morning before leaving the hotel, we checked the weather and prayed for the rain to disappear. We prayed for gentle hills and merciful winds. Two of those prayers were answered as requested.

After service, we ate a few Kind bars and vowed to each other that we were going to press through the rain all the way to our first planned stop in Ludowici. Nineteen hard miles of cold rain, gentle hills, almost no wind and very kind motorists took us to our first stop.

I went inside the Parker's gas station and ordered us two large coffees. We took our time enjoying them with more snacks. The cold rain was almost a surprise blessing, acting as a continuous cold compress for our joints and muscles as it soaked through our clothes. We finished the coffee, checked the map and pressed on fourteen more miles to our destination for the night, Days Inn of Jesup.

Friends, I don't know if I've ever felt more accomplished than battling through those thirty-three miles today.

I'm reminded of *Romans 5:3-4* "Not only so, suffering produces perseverance; perseverance, character; and character hope."

Today's joyful suffering has filled countless cups of hope that, together with God's steadfast love, I can take on any challenge ahead. I can't wait to see what challenging adventures in ministry God has waiting for me.

Shivering in Ludowici, GA

Conn (left), Jeremy (right)

FEBRUARY 17, 2020 (AM)

1 John 4:18

*18 There is no fear in love. But perfect love drives out
fear, because fear has to do with punishment.
The one who fears is not made perfect in love.*

Thank you Lord for another night of rest. We're almost to the end of this sabbath journey, and I thank you again for the grand blessing it has been. Thank you for your word this morning that is affirming your unfailing love, strength and vision for the day ahead. I ask your blessing of safety as we travel today. I pray again for merciful winds and gentle hills.

Thank you Lord for another day.

FEBRUARY 17, 2020 (PM)

Psalm 119:105

[105] *Your word is a lamp for my feet,*
a light on my path.

Lord, your word has nourished and energized me the whole way here. Five days Lord. Five Days of challenge, joy, blessings and energized hope to get through. Thank you for the smooth ride today in which I was able to focus more on you and spend time speaking with you. Lord thank you for speaking to me on this journey. I'm ready for what you have for me.

We woke early today at 6:00 am and enjoyed the hotel breakfast buffet. We were ready and on the road by 8:00 am. We started the ride with a slight drizzle that ended quickly. We pressed hard for nineteen miles down US 301 for Hortense.

In Hortense, we refueled with snacks and hydration. From there, we headed east on GA 32 for Atkinson.

We were hoping to get milkshakes at The Village Snack Bar, but they are closed on Mondays. So, we went across the street to Satilla Grocery. Our gears and chains had been crunching loudly from the toll of rain and sandy dirt roads. After a few BBQ sandwiches, we lubed up both bikes and continued the day's journey east on US 82 for twelve more miles. Those twelve miles were the longest.

Moderate wind and a few hills slowed us down, but not by much. While riding the shoulder, I picked up a piece of aluminum fencing in my rear hub but caught it quickly before it could cause any damage. I don't ride the shoulder anymore.

We pressed on again for thirty minutes to arrive just before 2:00 pm. We walked our bikes down the trail at the entrance to The Hostel in The Forest and were immediately enchanted. We parked our bikes next to the Dome check-in-house where Allison checked us in and gave us a tour. We settled into our tree house, took showers, explored the property and started winding down before dinner.

This journey has been so much more than I expected. God has given strength, focus and hope the whole way through. Tomorrow is the last day. We're going home. I'll miss this, but I'm refueled and ready for the challenges ahead. Thirty-three miles left.

East of Hortense, Ga

Entrance to Hostel in the Forest, Brunswick, Ga

Home for the night at Hostel in the Forest, Brunswick, Ga

Leaving Hostel in the Forest, Brunswick, Ga.
Jeremy (left), Conn (right).

FEBRUARY 18, 2020 (AM)

Philippians 4:8-13

[8] Finally, brothers and sisters, whatever is true, whatever is noble, whatever is right, whatever is pure, whatever is lovely, whatever is admirable—if anything is excellent or praiseworthy—think about such things.
[9] Whatever you have learned or received or heard from me, or seen in me—put it into practice.
And the God of peace will be with you.
[10] I rejoiced greatly in the Lord that at last you renewed your concern for me. Indeed, you were concerned, but you had no opportunity to show it. [11] I am not saying this because I am in need, for I have learned to be content whatever the circumstances. [12] I know what it is to be in need, and I know what it is to have plenty. I have learned the secret of being content in any and every situation, whether well fed or hungry, whether living in plenty or in want. [13] I can do all this through him who gives me strength.
Colossians 3:12-14

[12] Therefore, as God's chosen people, holy and dearly loved, clothe yourselves with compassion, kindness, humility, gentleness and patience. [13] Bear with each other and forgive one another if any of you has a grievance against someone. Forgive as the Lord forgave

37

you. [14] *And over all these virtues put on love, which*
binds them all together in perfect unity.

Today we finish. Lord, thank you for this journey. Thank
you for strength, guidance, love, hope and safety. Thank you
for generous friends along the way. I ask your blessing over
these last thirty-three miles. Give us strength, safety and fair
weather. Focus our hearts to you once again.

What an amazing time at The Hostel in the Forest. We
explored the grounds, drank coffee and enjoyed fireside
fellowship before dinner. During dinner, we got to hear
introductions and gratitude from everyone here. Then we
enjoyed a meal together. The manager sprung for pizza and
paired it with a hand-picked salad from the garden. We also
had green papaya kimchi which I'll be trying to make when
I get home. Staying here reminds me of one of my old
favorite songs by Chris Rice called "My Cathedral."

The Hostel in the Forest.

What a beautiful place to experience God's creation.

FEBRUARY 18, 2020 (PM)

James 1:2-4

² Consider it pure joy, my brothers and sisters, whenever you face trials of many kinds, ³ because you know that the testing of your faith produces perseverance. ⁴ Let perseverance finish its work so that you may be mature and complete, not lacking anything.

We left close to 10:00 am after taking our time with coffee and thanking our hosts at The Hostel in The Forest. From there we headed to the Exit 29 Waffle House where we both ordered an All-Star Breakfast. After charging up with a great breakfast, we pressed hard down US 17 to the Waverly Minit Mart.

Jay said Thursday, "I'll see you on the return trip."

I couldn't let him down. We enjoyed some cold sparkling water and pressed on hard to Woodbine, anxiously awaiting the bridge climb over the Satilla River.

We made it! I even had a decent break in traffic to snap a picture at the top of the bridge. From there we connected on the East Coast Greenway that parallels US 17 through Woodbine after taking a short rest. We pressed hard again now for Kingsland, only twelve miles to go. We took two short rests and arrived just after 2:00 pm.

What a day!

What a finish!

What an amazing journey!

These six days and 285 miles of joy, discover, and challenge have been a blessing beyond my possible imagination. Each time; through wind, hills, dirt roads, rain, aches and pains; I only made it through each challenge because God carried me. Along the way we were blessed with generous friends, beautiful scenery and mile after mile of quiet time with God.

This six-day journey is complete, but the next chapter of my journey in faith is just beginning. God has revealed to me that there is nothing I can't overcome if I have his overcoming love and strength with me. If I abide in His word and prayerful devotion every day, I'll be ready for any challenge ahead.

I'm so thankful for the support of my friends, family and dedicated fellow traveler Conn. I'm charged and ready to keep pressing forward in the journey God has for me ahead.

Blessings to you all on your journey and may the unfailing love of Christ be with you every step of the way.

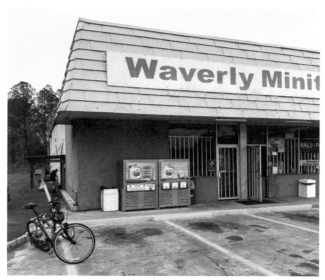

The hub of North Camden County activity,
The Waverly Minit Mart, Waverly, Ga

Satilla River Bridge, Woodbine, Ga

Arrival at Kingsland First UMC, Kingsland, Ga

Celebrating with an ice-cold sparkling water.
Jeremy (left) Conn (right).

ABOUT THE AUTHOR

Jeremy Cole is a six-year veteran youth pastor in St. Marys, Georgia. He enjoys traveling, camping, fishing, gardening and cooking. While not enjoying time outdoors, Jeremy spends time with his wife Amber and their foster children, as well as their two dogs Belle and Trinity. Jeremy is a long-time resident of St. Marys, Georgia and proudly serves in the same church in which he grew up, St. Marys United Methodist.

CPSIA information can be obtained
at www.ICGtesting.com
Printed in the USA
LVHW071530110421
684165LV00015B/38